A Wellbeing Journey

Middle School

Title: A Wellbeing Journey Middle School
ISBN: 9781957136950

Editors: Janna Nobleza and Elisa Flammini

Published 2023 by Seltrove, an imprint of Edtrove
Copyright Edtrove Ltd. and IB Source, Inc.

All rights reserved. No part of this publication may be copied or reproduced, stored in a retrieval system or transmitted in any form or by any means (electronic, mechanical, micro copying, photocopying, recording or otherwise), without prior written permission of the publishers.

The authors and publishers have made all efforts to ensure the accuracy and completeness of the information contained in this publication. No responsibility can be accepted for any errors, omissions, and/or inaccuracies that occur and any loss or damage suffered as a result.

Table of Contents

The Ingredients Of Me	1-2
Identity Iceberg	3
The Identity Code	4
More Than An Emoji	5-6
The Truth About Emotions	7
The Great Big Mix	8
Managing My Emotions	9-10
I'm In Control	11-12
Cross My Heart	13-14
Grow Your Mind	15
Keep Growing	16
Ready, Set, Go!	17-18
Let's Be Friends	19
Peer Pressure	20
Healthy Friendships	21-22
Sympathy & Empathy	23-24
Negative Peer Pressure	25-26
Boundaries	27-28
Yes, No, And Maybe?	29-30
Dealing With The Bully	31-32
Being An Upstander	33
Keep Bouncing	34
Think Before You Speak	35-36
Handling Setbacks	37-38
Help! I Need Somebody	39
Understanding Differences	40
Celebrating Diversity	41-42
Mirrors And Windows	43-44
Do You See What I See?	45
The Keeping Of Friends	46
Dealing With Conflict	47
Walking The Peace Path	48
Teamwork Makes The Dream Work	49-50
Can You Hear Me?	51-52
Everyone Belongs	53
Let's Hear It For Everyone!	54
Mindfulness	55-56
A Daily Mindfulness Practice	57-58
You Are Important	59-60
Gratitude	61-62
Coping Skills	63
Healthy Mind, Body, Heart	64
Decisions, Decisions!	65-66
Making The Tough Call	67-68
The Ripple Effect	69-70
Find Your Balance	71
Using Technology	72
Mistakes Stretch And Grow Us	73-74
Your Strengths	75-76
Leaders	77-78

Journal Prompts

Self-Awareness	81-82
Self-Management	83-83
Relationship Skills	85-86
Social Awareness	87-88
Responsible Decision-Making	89-90

Projects	89-95
Assessments	97-101

Skills Map

Self-Awareness

The Ingredients Of Me	1-2
Identity Iceberg	3
More Than An Emoji	5-6
The Truth About Emotions	7
Cross My Heart	13-14
Grow Your Mind	15
Keep Growing	16
You Are Important	59-60
Mistakes Stretch & Grow Us	73-74
Your Strengths	75-76

Social Awareness

Sympathy & Empathy	23-24
Celebrating Diversity	41-42
Understanding Differences	40
Mirrors And Windows	43-44
Do You See What I See?	45
Walking The Peace Path	48
Can You Hear Me?	51-52
Everyone Belongs	53
Gratitude	61-62

Self-Management

The Identity Code	4
The Great Big Mix	8
Managing My Emotions	9-10
I'm In Control	11-12
Ready, Set, Go!	17-18
Keep Bouncing	34
Handling Setbacks	37-38
Mindfulness	55-56
A Daily Mindfulness Practice	57-58
Coping Skills	63

Responsible Decision-Making

Negative Peer Pressure	25-26
Boundaries	27-28
Yes, No, And Maybe?	29-30
Dealing With The Bully	31-32
Dealing With Conflict	47
Decisions, Decisions	65-66
Making the Tough Call	66-67
The Ripple Effect	67-68
Healthy Mind, Body, & Heart	64
Find Your Balance	71
Using Technology	72

Relationship Skills

Let's be Friends	19
Peer Pressure	20
Healthy Friendships	21-22
Being An Upstander	33
Think Before You Speak	35-36
Help! I Need Somebody!	39
The Keeping Of Friends	46
Teamwork Makes The Dream Work	49-50
Let's Hear It For Everyone!	54
Strong, Confident Leaders	77-78

Journal Prompts

Self-Awareness	81-82
Self-Management	83-83
Relationship Skills	85-86
Social Awareness	87-88
Responsible Decision-Making	89-90

Hello!

Wellbeing focuses on who you are as an individual and your relationships you have with the people and world around you.

Research shows that people who build strong skills in the areas of social and emotional wellbeing are
- more likely to succeed in school
- better able to make responsible, healthy decisions
- more positive and have an optimistic look on life

To begin, simply pick a journal prompt, activity, or project based on the amount of time you have to spend.

Looking for more guidance? Our Teacher Guide and Parent Guide can help. Find it at www.myibsource.com.

Fill in Your Personal Info

YOUR NAME: _____

YOUR BIRTHDAY: _____

YOUR SELF-PORTRAIT

The Ingredients Of Me

Your identity is the personality traits you possess and your beliefs.

You may look to your friends, social media, and celebrities to find cues as to what you like, what you think or feel about various topics, and how to dress. This may inform part of your identity.

Reflection

- Who is really important to you?

- What activities do you enjoy?

- What do you like best about yourself?

- What do you hope for the future?

When you are consistent with who you are, others will recognize you by your character and personality and respect you as an individual.

If you had an ingredients label that describes who you are, what would it say? Make a label for yourself that tells what you are made of.

Ingredients:

Identity Iceberg

Fill the iceberg below with words that describe you following the directions below.

Top of the Iceberg: What people can see about your identity.

Below the water: What others may not be able to tell about you at first sight.

The water: Your environment since you behave differently in different places and with different people.

The Identity Code

Did you know that your identity is like your own personal brand, and it doesn't change no matter where you are? But how you act, talk, and even hold yourself can change depending on who you're with and where you're at.

It's called code-switching, like being a chameleon and changing colors to fit in with different surroundings. For example, you might act differently with your friends than your parents or grandparents. And you might talk differently at a dance than at a place of worship or home.

Practice code-switching in different environments by writing what you would say to each of the following people for each situation.

	A friend	Parent/ Carer	Teacher or Coach
You need to ask for a favor.			
You are feeling down and need encouragement.			

_____
_____
_____

4

More Than An Emoji

We often define emotions by "liking or disliking" statements or photos, clicking a ♥, or sharing a face to show how we feel. But are we genuinely communicating our emotions to others in a way that they understand?

Our emotions are more complex than this and sometimes feel confusing. Complex emotions require us to stop and think about our feelings and reflect on what is happening. For example, when we feel overwhelmed, we may feel BOTH powerless and defeated. These complexities make it difficult to express ourselves and to understand the emotions of others.

Look over the following complex emotions. What emotions make up these more complex ones? The first has been done for you.

Overwhelmed =   powerless + defeated

Confused = _____ + _____

Frustrated = _____ + _____

Depressed = _____ + _____

Jealous = _____ + _____

Disappointed = _____ + _____

Stress = _____ + _____

Guilty = _____ + _____

Annoyed = _____ + _____

Pick one of the complex emotions to focus on for this activity. Then, using magazine pictures, photos from the internet, or your own drawings to create a poster showing how your selected complex emotion may feel and look like in your body.

When your project is complete, answer the reflection questions below.

> If you were to give your project a title, what would you name it?

_____

_____

> Explain the types of images, words, and colors you used in your poster. How do these all showcase your selected emotion?

_____

_____

_____

> When you are feeling this emotion, what can you do to cope?

_____

_____

_____

The Truth About Emotions

Did you know that there are no good or bad emotions? Emotions are just feelings. You are not bad if you feel certain emotions. Practice reflecting on the emotions below.

Angry

What do you look like when you're angry? _____
_____

How do you feel when you're angry? _____
_____

Lonely

What do you look like when you're lonely? _____
_____

How do you feel when you're lonely? _____
_____

Emotion: _____

What do you look like when you're _____? _____
_____

How do you feel when you're _____? _____
_____

The Great Big Mix

Your emotions get more complex, mixed up, and complicated as you grow. It can sometimes be confusing to understand precisely how you feel when your emotions are all mixed up. Practice working with mixed emotions by talking through the following situations.

For each situation, think:
- How would I respond?
- What different emotions would I have?
- What makes this situation difficult?

You help a friend prepare for an academic competition. Your friend wins and is interviewed by the local news station and they don't even mention you and how you helped them prepare. They never thank you.

 You have to be at school early. On the way to school, you realize you forgot something you need. If you go back to get it, you will be late.

It's late and you are studying for a test. Your friend sends you a text saying they are really upset and need to talk.

Managing My Emotions

As you are learning, emotions aren't good or bad, they are just feelings. But that doesn't mean it is always easy to understand your emotions or to manage them.

People express emotions differently. For example, someone who is mad might scream and another person might withdraw when angry.

Think through how you feel, what you look like, and what others may see when you experience the emotions below.

Angry:

Sad:

Stressed:

Excited:

Create an emotional management kit with different ways you can calm your emotions when they get really intense. Put a strategy you could use in each of the pieces of the pie.

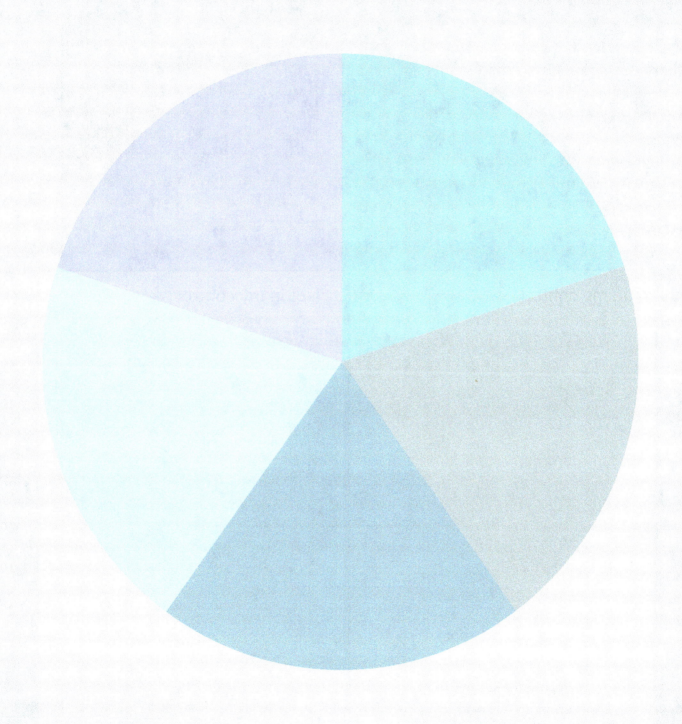

I'm In Control

You can manage your emotions better when you can let go of the things you cannot control and manage the things you can control.

Look over the following items and write them in the columns below based on whether it is something you control or can't control.

- Your height
- What you eat for dinner
- Your grades
- The mood of your teacher
- An F on a test
- The time you go to bed
- How long you exercise
- How busy you are

In my control	Not in my control

Let go of the things you can't control and manage your emotions for the things you can control.

Did you find that you control or didn't control most things on the list?

Were there some things that you felt were a little of both? How so?

What are some ways you can let go of the things that you don't have control over?

Cross My Heart

Being honest seems so simple: just tell the truth. But it can easily become complicated and messy.

What may complicate being honest?

_____
_____
_____
_____

Being honest can be hard. You must be brave and confident to be honest with yourself and others.

What are some ways you can ensure you are honest with yourself?

_____
_____
_____
_____

When you are honest with others, you can still be kind. Consider what to say, what tone of voice to use, and when to speak.

Follow the journey below and fill in the blanks to learn more about honesty.

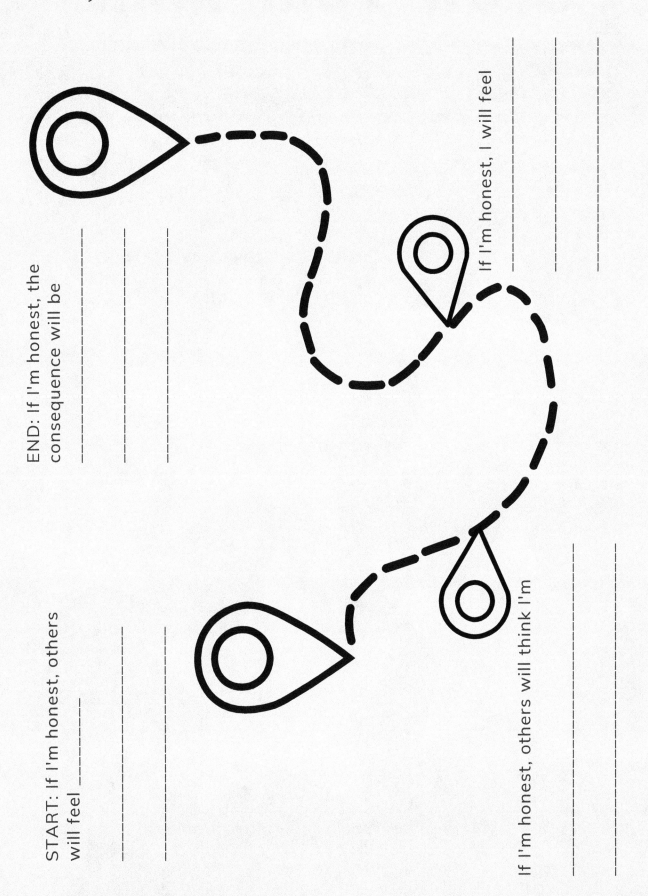

START: If I'm honest, others will feel _____

If I'm honest, others will think I'm _____

If I'm honest, I will feel _____

END: If I'm honest, the consequence will be _____

Grow Your Mind

When you think, "I can't do this," you begin believing what you say to yourself. Many times this makes your statement come true. When you say encouraging things to yourself, you train your brain to be more positive.

Fill in the stars below with encouraging and caring things you can say to yourself to lift yourself up & gain confidence.

Remember, be kind and compassionate with yourself, and focus on your strengths and potential. You got this!

Keep Growing

You can use a growth mindset to help you through problems and intense emotions. A growth mindset is a frame of mind examining what is possible. A growth mindset can make you resilient and more successful. Practice changing a fixed mindset into a growth mindset below.

Fixed Mindset	Growth Mindset
I'll never make the team	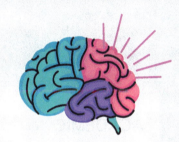
My teacher never helps me. 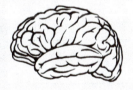	
I will never finish all this homework!	
The coach never puts me in. I'll only be a benchwarmer this season	
Why do we have to read books written 100 years ago? They don't make any sense.	

Ready, Set, Go!

Goals challenge you, inspire you, and give you focus and purpose. When you make a goal, remember that your goal should be SMART. This stands for:

S	**M**	**A**	**R**	**T**
Specific	Measurable	Attainable	Relevant	Timely

What goals do you have? Fill in the activity below.

ACADEMIC

I will be able to _____

_____

By the time of _____

I will reach this goal by _____

_____

_____

I am excited to work on this goal because _____

_____

_____

PASSION

I will be able to _____

_____

By the time of _____

I will reach this goal by _____

_____

_____

I am excited to work on this goal because _____

_____

_____

WELLNESS

I will be able to _____

_____

By the time of _____

I will reach this goal by _____

_____

_____

I am excited to work on this goal because _____

_____

_____

Let's Be Friends

Reflect on friendships you have, or have had, and the relationships you may have observed. Think about what friendship means, how you are as a friend, and what you need in a friendship.

What kind of friend am I? What are the best qualities I can give to someone as a friend?

What do I see in others' friendships that I would like to have in a friend?

What qualities are important to me in a friend?

What are some of the best times or memories I have had with friends that brought us closer?

Peer Pressure

Peer pressure is when others strongly influence or encourage you to do things, whether it's positive or negative. How can you match the types of peer pressure with each situation?

Your team has a final practice before a match, and even though it's optional, you know that all your teammates will be going. You don't want to go but you would disappoint your team by not showing up.

Unspoken negative peer pressure

You and your friend get into an argument and everyone around you starts yelling, "Fight!".

Spoken negative peer pressure

You wear your favorite jersey to school and your friends give you a disgusted look and don't sit with you at lunch.

Unspoken positive peer pressure

You hang out with your friend after school and they say, "Let's study for our test tomorrow first." So you study.

Spoken positive peer pressure

When you feel negative peer pressure, what can you do?

Healthy Friendships

Friendships can either be healthy or unhealthy, depending on how they are built and maintained. Can you think of some examples describing the difference between a healthy friendship and an unhealthy one?

A healthy friendship may look like this...	A unhealthy friendship may look like this...

One way to maintain healthy relationships is to have boundaries - things that you know will not make you happy and you can not deal with. What are your boundaries?

MY BOUNDARIES:

ACTIONS:

MY BOUNDARIES	ACTIONS
Gossiping behind my back	Confront the person assertively and explain that I cannot tolerate this in a friendship. I wish them the best and remain polite when interacting with them in the future.

Sympathy vs Empathy

Sympathy is when you feel sorry for someone and want them to feel better.

On the other hand, empathy is when you try to understand what someone is going through and support the person through their experience.

Can you tell which scenario shows sympathy and which one shows empathy?

Your friend's parents are getting divorced. You say, "I'm so sorry to hear that."	Sympathy	Empathy
Your little brother loses his drone after a large burst of wind comes through. You put your arm around his shoulders and say, "Oh, that's devastating." You then sit with him and give him a hug.	Sympathy	Empathy
Your teacher says her pet died last night. You say, "I'm so sorry. Is there anything I can do to help?"	Sympathy	Empathy

It can be easy to use sympathy. Empathy can be harder. Write a picture book teaching younger children how to use empathy. You can use one of the idea starters below or create your own idea for your story.

When you're done with your picture book, volunteer to read your book to a preschool or young elementary classroom, as you can see, sympathy is nice, but empathy is even better.

Story Ideas:

- Your sibling is having a bad day and is taking it out on everyone, including you! They might be yelling or being mean.

- Your friend invites you over to their house, but doesn't invite your other friend who is standing next to you.

- On the playground, you see a young child who has fallen down and scraped their knee. They are crying.

Negative Peer Pressure

Peer pressure is when other people around you strongly encourage or influence you to do things, even if you don't want to, just to fit in or gain their approval. Now, let's work together with a classmate or small group to answer these questions:

What are some of the examples of peer pressure that teenagers face?

What are the consequences of these social pressures? Are there school consequences? Personal ones?

Why might peer pressure be more powerful at this age than for younger children?

What can you do when you are feeling pressured into something you don't want to do?

With your same classmates or small group, think through some real-life consequences to the following examples, and then create your own real-life situation to reflect on.

Using substances such as vapes, drugs or alcohol

Cheating on a test

Post certain pictures on social media

_____
_____

Boundaries

A boundary is a personal limit you establish for yourself and your relationships. You can control your body, the physical space around you, and the decisions you make. Read through the following situation. What advice would you give this student?

> *Lately, life has been really good. The person I had a crush on likes me back and we started dating. I like them a lot and I like spending time with them. But now that we are together, they often come up to me and hug me while I'm talking to my friends. It makes me feel uncomfortable because sometimes I need my own space. How can I show them I want to be with them, but also need time on my own with my friends?*

What advice would you give this person?

_____
_____
_____
_____
_____
_____
_____

> Did you know that personal boundaries are:
> 1. Self-created
> 2. Need to be respected
> 3. Can change over time

In a small group, pick a scenario where a boundary is needed. Then create a quick skit showing the situation and how the person created a boundary. Once you have your skit set, present it in front of another small group or your class.

If you're struggling thinking of a situation, you can pick one from below.

- You go to a party and are expected to drink, but you don't want to.

- Your friend is failing science and is trying to copy your homework.

- Your group of friends are at a store and are shoplifting. You don't feel comfortable stealing or staying with them at the store anymore.

- There is a bridge that everyone tags and late at night, you and your friends decide to go tag it too. But as you get there, you realize you don't want to anymore; you know it's wrong.

Yes, No, And Maybe

Consent is another word for permission. It is essential to ask for consent from other people and it's important that other people ask for consent from you. When giving or receiving consent, it's important to remember FRIES.

Consent is:

Freely given
Reversible
Informed
Enthusiastically given
Specific

How does it feel when someone asks your permission before touching you or using something you own?

Have you ever given consent, but you didn't really want to? What happened? How did you feel?

Look through the following list. Circle where the person is giving consent.

Yes!	Nods their head.
Maybe in a bit.	I'm not sure.
No thanks.	Shakes their head.
No answer; silence.	Ok!

Read through each scenario. Can you determine if consent is given?

> You want to use your friend's phone. You've used it before and they aren't using it right now, so you pick it up.

> Your friend is sad and you want to give them a hug. You say, "Can I give you a hug?" They nod their head and unfold their arms so you can hug them.

> You're at a party and give a drink to the person you're with, but they say, "ummm" but they take the glass you are holding out.

> You are walking down the hall and see your friend. You grab their hand to hold, but they try to take their hand back. They don't say no.

Dealing With The Bully

Bullying is unwanted, aggressive behavior among school aged children that involves a real or perceived power imbalance. The behavior is repeated, or has the potential to be repeated, over time.

If you witness bullying and take action to stop it, you're called an <u>upstander</u>. However, you're called a <u>bystander</u> if you don't do anything to help.

> Bullying tends to be most common during middle school and doesn't increase during high school. Remember, being kind and standing up for what's right is always better.

A graphic novel uses pictures, words, and speech/thought bubbles to tell a story. Read through the following story and create a short graphic novel showing what is happening and what you can do to be an upstander.

> Mana is Muslim. In gym class the students have started a unit on swimming, but Mana is not allowed to join due to her religious beliefs. Her teachers has given her writing assignments instead, but as she sits and works on them, students splash water her way every day when the teacher isn't looking. As they splash, they intentionally try to get her headscarf wet and make her feel uncomfortable.

Title: _____

Being An Upstander

An upstander is someone who takes action to stop bullying. You show bravery and compassion when you stand up for others and speak out against what is wrong. There are many ways that you can be an upstander and help others With a small group, make a list of some of the ways you could be an upstander.

- _____
- _____
- _____
- _____
- _____

How have you been a brave upstander before? _____

_____

_____

Have you ever seen someone else be an upstander? What did you notice?

_____

_____

_____

An upstander is brave and protects others... just like a superhero!

Keep Bouncing

When you're playing basketball, the first thing you do is pick a ball. You want to find one that's full of air and bounces well. If a ball has lost some air, it will be squishy and won't bounce as high. Resilience is like a ball's ability to bounce back. You can see the difference in resilience by how hard you bounce the ball. The harder you push it down, the higher it will bounce back up.

Of course, you're not a basketball, but you're still resilient. You face pressures and stresses like peer pressure, homework, expectations, and goals that can push you down. Just like basketballs are filled with air to make them more resilient, what are you filled with that makes you resilient?

Think about what helps you bounce back from tough times and write down your thoughts in the space below.

Think Before You Speak

Words have a lot of power. They can heal wounds and they can hurt others (and yourself). Read through this example to see just how powerful words can be:

In a science experiment, Emoto froze water crystals in two jars. He spoke loving words to one jar and hurtful words to the other daily. After some time, he examined the ice crystals under a microscope.

The water crystals that received loving words transformed into beautiful snowflake crystals with six symmetrical sides, and they sparkled brilliantly.

On the other hand, the water crystals that were exposed to negative, hurtful words were uneven, dark, and dull.

Before you speak, THINK:
T - Is it True?
H - Is it Helpful?
I - Is it Inspiring?
N - Is it Necessary?
K - Is it Kind?

Spend some time reflecting and thinking about the way you use your own words.

Think of a time you said something to a friend you wish you hadn't said.	Think of a time you said something to yourself that you wish you hadn't thought.
Was is True?	Was is True?
Was is Helpful?	Was is Helpful?
Was it Inspiring?	Was it Inspiring?
Was it Necessary?	Was it Necessary?
Was it Kind?	Was it Kind?
What could you have said or done instead?	What could you have said to yourself instead?

Handling Setbacks

It's normal to feel disappointed or discouraged sometimes and want to give up. However, it's essential to understand that failure is a valuable experience. Your failures can teach you a lot and help you become more resilient. When you face setbacks or failures, it's an opportunity to bounce back and develop grit, which means having the strength and perseverance to keep going even when things get tough.

Remember, setbacks and failures are a natural part of life and you're not alone in experiencing them. Below you will find a list of celebrities and famous people. Pick two people and research their stories of failure and resiliency.

Answer the questions about the celebrities you chose:
- How did they triumph even after facing setbacks?
- What can you learn from their experiences?

- Taylor Swift
- J.K. Rowling
- Lizzo
- Lady Gaga
- Lebron James

- Albert Einstein
- Selena Gomez
- Bill Gates
- Tom Holland
- Marie Curie

- _____

1 _____

How did this person triumph even after facing setbacks?

_____
_____
_____

What can you learn from their experience?

_____
_____
_____

2 _____

How did this person triumph even after facing setbacks?

_____
_____
_____

What can you learn from their experience?

_____
_____
_____

Help! I Need Somebody

Asking for help is a courageous act, not a weakness. When you ask for help; it shows that you're not giving up and that you're willing to face challenges and obstacles head-on.

How might asking for help be a way to develop resilience?

Who can help you when you are struggling? Fill in the activity below to remind yourself of the people who are there for you.

Name:
When can you go to them for help?

Name:
When can you go to them for help?

Name:
When can you go to them for help?

Understanding Differences

Each of us has our own unique story about where we come from, and it's essential to share our stories with others and listen to theirs in return. Some ways that people categories differences include
- race
- religion
- nationality
- sexuality
- cultures
- abilities
- gender
- family structures

In a small group, discuss the following questions. As you listen to your group members' answers, be open-minded and practice listening with empathy.

- What are some differences that divide people?

- What are some common differences that may prevent people from getting to know each other? Why?

- Have you resisted interacting with someone because they were different? What were your thoughts?

- How can you apply a growth mindset to include others who are different from yourself?

Celebrating Diversity

Celebrating diversity means being excited and interested in learning about different cultures and experiences that are different from our own. When we connect with people who are different, it's essential to keep an open mind and be accepting of everyone. We all want to feel like we belong and be able to connect with others.

One way to learn how to celebrate diversity is to start by exploring your uniqueness and background. Try the following activity to reflect on your own experiences.

This is how I would describe my...

- Race and ethnicity

- Culture

- Family

- Relationships

- Holidays and traditions

Now that you have reflected on your own experience, find a partner and learn about their experience.

My partner: _____

From my partner, I learned...

- Race and ethnicity

- Culture

- Family

- Relationships

- Holidays and traditions

- We are similar because...

- We are different because...

Mirrors And Windows

As you learn about diversity, you can think about two different ideas: mirrors and windows.

A mirror is when what you are learning, listening to, watching, or reading is reflecting back a similar experience you have had.

_____
_____
_____
_____

A window opens up an experience that is new or different than your own.

_____
_____
_____
_____

We need both mirrors and windows to fully celebrate diversity and be inclusive.

Let's practice by playing bingo. To play, you must get three in a row. Read through each box and see if you can get a bingo. You cannot use a book more than once!

A book where the main character was really similar to me! Title: _____ Name of the character: _____	A book where the action took place in a country different from mine. Title: _____ Country in the book: _____	A book where I learned something new. Title: _____ What I learned: _____ _____
A book that made me feel curious to learn more. Title: _____ What I want to learn: _____	A book that made me feel good about myself. Title: _____ What made me feel good: _____ _____	A book where the main character was really different from me! Title: _____ Name of the character: _____
A book that was set in a different time period. Title: _____ Time period: _____	A book where the character was like me but also different. Title: _____ Name of the character: _____	A book where the family structure was different from mine. Title: _____ Family differences: _____ _____

Do You See What I See?

Perspective-taking means seeing things from someone else's point of view. To do this, you have to try to imagine what it's like to be in their situation and think about how you would feel, think, or act if you were in their shoes.

> Have you ever watched a game on TV and there was a review of the play to find out what the call should be?

Before they review the play, did you agree or disagree with the referee? Why?

_____

_____

_____

What did you see that the referee perhaps didn't see?

_____

_____

_____

The referee could only consider their point of view. When reviewing a play in ports, the reviewers have access to multiple camera angles to see every aspect of the play. This helps them make a more informed decision about what the call should be.

The review's outcome can either confirm the original call made by the referee or overturn it based on the additional perspectives available.

The Keeping Of Friends

It is normal to make friends, and then lose or fall out of touch with each other sometimes. This is a common struggle that many people go through, so you're not alone in feeling this way.

You probably already know that many factors contribute to maintaining long-lasting friendships. Being a compassionate and supportive friend is one of them.

Practice perspective-taking and empathy by giving advice to the following student.

I made the decision to join the school band this year and I'm really enjoying it! However, my best friend isn't part of the band and has no interest in joining. As a result, I feel like we're growing apart since I have to practice after school frequently. We don't have as much free time to spend together anymore. I'm worried about our friendship and want to know what I can do to keep it going.

Dealing With Conflict

Conflicts are part of life. Whenever we interact with someone, there is a potential for conflict because people's needs and expectations differ.

Can you think of ways you can deal with conflict?

1. _____
2. _____
3. _____
4. _____

Read through the following situations. How could you resolve the conflict?

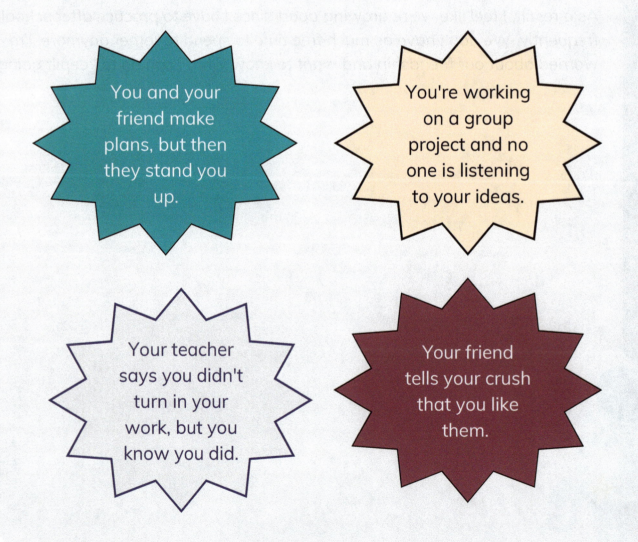

- You and your friend make plans, but then they stand you up.
- You're working on a group project and no one is listening to your ideas.
- Your teacher says you didn't turn in your work, but you know you did.
- Your friend tells your crush that you like them.

Walking The Peace Path

One way to solve conflicts is by using I statements. You can try it by filling in the blanks below.

Think of a time when you and a friend were disagreeing. Use the I statement formula below to solve the problem.

I feel _____

when _____

_____

_____

I need _____

_____

would you be willing to _____

_____

_____

Teamwork Makes The Dream Work

Regarding working in groups, some people love it, and others hate it. There are some advantages to working in a group, such as being able to bounce ideas off each other and getting help with a big project. However, it can be uncomfortable and challenging sometimes, especially if everyone has different ideas or personalities.

What do you think makes groups work the best?

- _____
- _____
- _____
- _____

Most likely, you have some collaboration on your list above. Collaboration is when everyone works together to accomplish a task or goal.

> Work with your classmates in a small group to solve a problem at school. It could be anything from improving security during lunchtime, deciding on a theme for the next dance, or finding ways to reduce congestion in the hallways. Get creative and come up with some solutions together!

49

Our Problem:

_____

_____

_____

Our Brainstorming:

Our Solution:

_____

_____

_____

Can You Hear Me?

Sometimes you may experience conflict because you have yet to listen (or be listened to) fully. Listening well to others is a way to show empathy, be a good friend, and be open-minded. Here is an example of reflective listening:

> I forgot my homework again today, so my teacher gave me detention. My mom is going to be so mad since I won't be able to go home on the bus and she will have to come pick me up.

Reflective listening response:

> Oh wow...it sounds like you are having a really bad day.

Notice that when you really listen, you aren't trying to give advice or tell the person how they were wrong. Instead, you reflect back on what they told you.

> I studied so hard for that test, but I ended up with a bad grade. I'm never going to pass this class.

In the lunch line they started talking about me even though they knew I could hear...and it wasn't very nice. I don't know why they can't just keep my name out of their mouth!

A situation in your life:

Everyone Belongs

Being able to include others who you don't know well or don't have much in common with is a great habit and can help everyone feel welcome.

What are some ways you can help others feel a sense of belonging?

- _____
- _____
- _____
- _____

Throughout this week, look for ways you can help others feel welcome and like they belong. Use some of the ways from your list. Write down what you did and how successful you think you were.

What did you do?	Were you successful?

Let's Hear It For Everyone!

You have probably been to a pep rally, football, or basketball game. When the pressure is on, and the team is down, the cheerleaders are screaming at the top of their voices...chanting and encouraging. Encouragement is empathy in action. Read through these quotations. Do they encourage you?

> It's hard to beat a person who never gives up."
> —Babe Ruth

> "All our dreams can come true, if we have the courage to pursue them."
> —Walt Disney

> "The hard days are what make you stronger."
> —Aly Raisman

In small groups, find an encouraging quotation and then make a poster that you can hang on the school wall to encourage other students. Use this checklist to keep you organized.

- ☐ Research and brainstorm quotations
- ☐ As a group decide on the one you want to focus on
- ☐ Decide on a design for the poster
- ☐ Write the quotation and create the poster
- ☐ Hang your poster in the classroom or school

Mindfulness

Mindfulness is the intentional practice of focusing and paying attention to your emotions and your environment.

Using mindfulness can...

- Recenter your focus.
- Manage your emotions.
- Improve your memory.
- Relieve stress.
- Sooth anxious thoughts.
- Lower sadness.
- Increase empathy for others.
- Calm your body.

One way to practice mindfulness is to sit quietly and be intentional about your breath. Pick one (or both) of the activities below to try it.

Hot Chocolate Breathing

Imagine you are holding a cup of hot chocolate, and you're blowing the little marshmallows around to cool your cup. Take in a deep breath through your nose and then exhale through your mouth to blow those tiny marshmallows around your cup. Repeat five times.

Hand Tracing Breathing

Use your pencil and trace your hand on this page (it's ok if you mark over the text). Now use your drawing to breathe in and out as you trace your fingers. Start below your thumb and as you trace the line up your thumb, breathe in. As you trace your thumb down toward your finger, breath out. Breathe in and out slowly as you trace up and down your fingers.

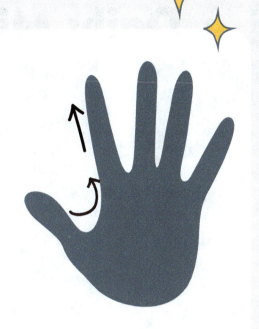

Reflection
How do you feel after doing a mindful breathing practice?

_____

_____

_____

_____

_____

A Daily Mindfulness Practice

Mindfulness enhances your ability to learn, manage your emotions, and calm your body. You can practice mindfulness by breathing, but you can also practice being mindful by:

- Spending time outside
- Journaling
- Setting intentions for your day
- Meditation or prayer
- A daily reflection routine

Day: _____

1. I'm grateful for
_____
_____

2. My hopes for today are _____
_____
_____

3. When I get stressed today, I'm going to
_____
_____

Day: _____

1. I'm grateful for
_____
_____

2. My hopes for today are _____
_____
_____

3. When I get stressed today, I'm going to
_____
_____

Day: _____

1. I'm grateful for
_____
_____

2. My hopes for today are _____
_____
_____

3. When I get stressed today, I'm going to
_____
_____

Day: _____

1. I'm grateful for
_____
_____

2. My hopes for today are _____
_____
_____

3. When I get stressed today, I'm going to
_____
_____

Day: _____

1. I'm grateful for
_____
_____

2. My hopes for today are _____
_____
_____

3. When I get stressed today, I'm going to
_____
_____

Day: _____

1. I'm grateful for
_____
_____

2. My hopes for today are _____
_____
_____

3. When I get stressed today, I'm going to
_____
_____

You Are Important

You may have heard about mental health and well-being in the news, but what does it mean? It's all about a person's emotional, psychological, and social wellness. This affects how they handle stress, their relationships, and their decisions. It's essential to prioritize your mental health, no matter your age.

Put a check in the box to mark your opinion. You may be surprised by the answers.

	Strongly disagree	Disagree	Agree	Strongly agree
Anyone can have a mental health problem.				
I would be too embarrassed to tell anyone that I had a mental health problem.				
People with mental health problems are violent.				
If I thought a friend had a mental health problem, I would stay away from them.				

	Strongly disagree	Disagree	Agree	Strongly agree
I have heard a person I know call someone names like 'nutter,' 'psycho,' 'loony.'				
If I thought that I had a mental health problem, I would talk to someone.				
Mental health problems only affect adults, not children and young people.				
Only certain kinds of people develop mental health problems.				

1. Anyone can experience a mental health problem. 1/4 people experience one in their life.
2. Embarrassment and fear of being stigmatized, is a major stumbling block for people who need help with a mental health problem. Yet, being able to talk to someone can help.
3. This is NOT true. This is a pervasive myth. People with mental health problems are much more likely to be victims of violence.
4. Sometimes friends feel that they don't know enough to be able to help or feel uncomfortable. You don't need to be an expert on mental health to be a friend.
5. Such language increases the stigma faced by people experiencing mental health problems and makes it more difficult for them to seek support.
6. A better understanding of mental health problems can reduce the fear, and it is often just very simple, ordinary things that you can do to help a friend.
7. Getting support is a VERY positive factor in treating mental health problems and promoting recovery. It's good to talk!
8. Children and young people may experience mental health problems.

Gratitude

Do you focus more on what you don't have? Do you always seem to be comparing yourself to others? It's easy to do, but it isn't helpful. Gratitude is another word for being thankful. Being grateful has been scientifically proven to increase happiness and well-being!

Can you think of some of the other benefits gratitude might have on your life?

Gratitude supports your physical, emotion, and mental wellbeing!

Practice gratitude by answering the prompts.

I am grateful for these 3...

Friends

Personal strengths

Family members

Things about my health/body

Achievements

Things I have at home

Coping Skills

Ever had a great morning, only to hit a roadblock later in the day?
It can be tough to know how to react. You have two choices: avoid the problem or struggle by getting upset, or COPE with it. Coping means taking a moment to make a healthy decision about how to deal with the issue.

Fill in the stop signs below with some ways you can cope with hard things.

Coping skills are the choices we make to deal with unexpected situations.

Healthy Mind, Body, Heart

By making healthy decisions, you can keep a healthy mind, body, and heart. Use the chart below to find ways to keep your mind, body, and heart healthy. Use the intersection of the circles to put things that keep two or all three of these things healthy.

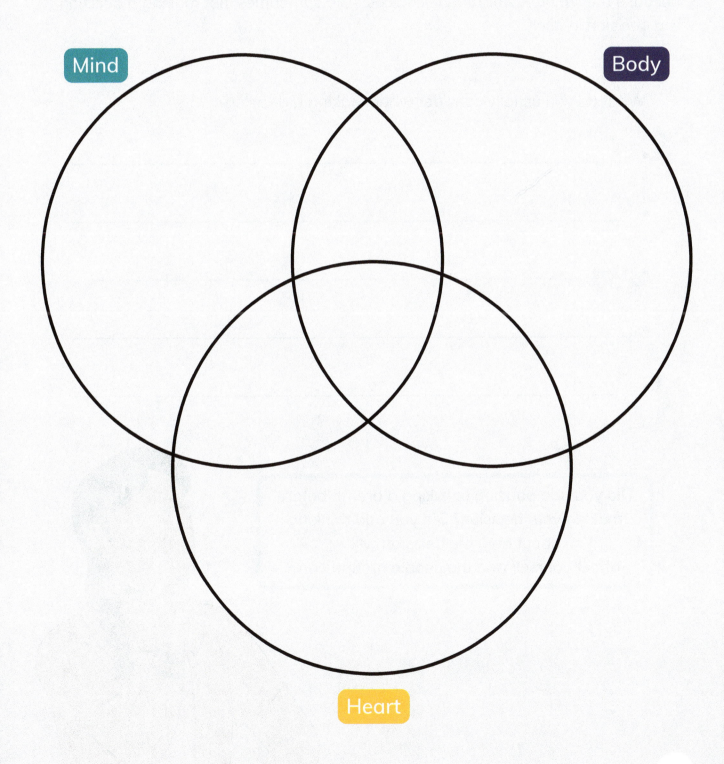

Decisions, Decisions!

Did you know that you make over **3,000** decisions every day? That's a lot! And out of those, about 200 are just about what to eat daily.
But here's the thing: most decisions are made without thinking about them because they're habits or routine choices. And sometimes, not making a decision is a decision in itself.

What do you usually consider when making a decision?

- _____
- _____
- _____
- _____
- _____

> Did you add pausing or taking a breath before making your decision? Did you add thinking about how the decision will affect yourself and the people around you?

Read through the following situations to decide what you would do. Can you make a healthy decision for yourself and others?

> You're at the movies and when it's over, a friend wants to sneak into another theatre to watch a different movie.

> You are at a party and someone gives you a plastic cup with alcohol in it.

> You are at the store trying on sunglasses and think it would be easy to put them in your pocket and leave the store.

> You didn't do your homework but your friend did. You have 10 minutes before class begins.

66

Making The Tough Call

Making decisions can be challenging. Especially if you're making a decision that could affect your future or your relationships.

What are some BIG decisions you have made in the past like this?

Using a step-by-step decision-making process can make it easier. When making a decision, do the following:

1. Identify the problem
2. Gather information
3. Brainstorm possible solutions
4. Identify possible consequences
5. Make a choice
6. Take action
7. Evaluate the outcome

Practice using this step-by-step decision-making process by filling out this activity below.

Identify the problem:
_____
_____

Gather information:
_____
_____

Brainstorm possible solutions:
_____
_____
_____

Identify possible consequences:
_____
_____
_____

Make a choice: _____
Take action!
Evaluate the outcome:
_____
_____

The Ripple Effect

Have you ever skipped stones before in a lake or river? What happens when the stone hits the water?

Those rings that appear when the stone disappears under the water are what we are talking about today: the ripple effect. When we make decisions (or make the decision NOT to do something), our decisions affect ourselves and others.

Can you think of a list of people who may feel the effects of your decisions?

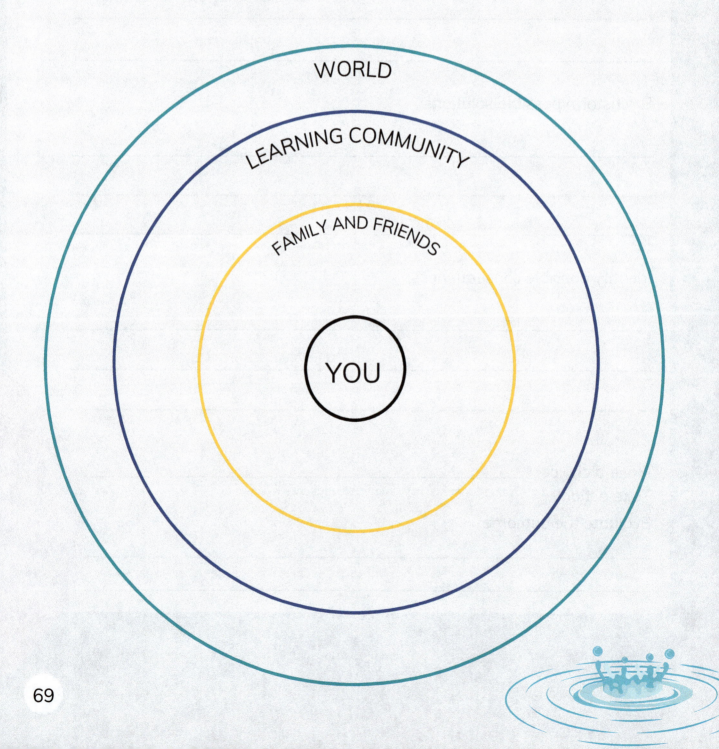

Let's look at an example. You may stay up late on your phone. You know this will affect you tomorrow. How might it affect your friends? Family? Teachers? Classmates?

_____

_____

_____

Using paper, write a decision you have made in the last month in the center. Then crunch it up so it's a paper ball. Do this for five different decisions.
Now take turns tossing your five paper balls into the bins that fit each decision best. Think about why you are making each choice.

> How does understanding that your decisions affect others, not just yourself, change your perspective? What might you do differently next time?

70

Find Your Balance

Learning how to ride a bike or skate requires balance and balance is also essential for your mental and emotional health.

For instance, while staying up late occasionally for things like finishing homework or hanging out with friends is okay, balance means not staying late every night.

How many hours do you participate in each activity? Add your activities in the blank spaces.

Sleeping	____ hours
Watching TV	____ hours
Playing Video Games	____ hours
Being on Social Media	____ hours
_____	____ hours
_____	____ hours
_____	____ hours
_____	____ hours

1. What areas do not look balanced?
2. What do you need to do more of?
3. What do you need to do less of?
4. What goal could you make to help yourself lead a more balanced and healthy life?

Using Technology

Screen time and using technology can have harmful effects, but there are also benefits. It's important to balance your use on screens so you can have a healthy mind, body, and heart.

Make a list of some of the harmful effects and benefits you see in your life when using technology.

Harmful effects	Benefits

Mistakes Stretch & Grow Us

Learning changes how your brain learns. It can be hard every time you learn something new because you are carving out a new path in your brain. There are things you can do when learning and making mistakes to make it easier.

Put a star next to your favorites below and try them next time learning is hard, or you make a mistake.

Tell yourself, "It's ok; I'm learning."	Apologize.
Be honest with yourself and others.	Forgive yourself.
Remind yourself all humans make mistakes.	Be patient with yourself.
Take a breath and try again.	Fix what you can.
Remember everyone make mistakes.	Know you are now closer at getting it right.

Remember when you make a mistake or things get hard, pause and take a deep breath.

Use this page to make a comic strip about someone making a mistake and dealing with it in a healthy way.

Title: _____

74

Your Strengths

Knowing your strengths allows you to tackle obstacles, find joy, and improve your overall well-being. Playing to your strengths improves teamwork, increases self-awareness, and can help you set goals.

Below is a list of different strengths. Go through each and CIRCLE the ones you possess.

Dedication	Teamwork skills
Perseverance	Computer skills
Outgoing	Strong writer
Good speaker	Good communicator
Open-minded	Organization
Inclusive	Positive
Respectful	Patient
Kind	Responsible
Trustworthy	Problem-solver
Caring	Leader

Now go back through the list and now put a star by the strengths you WANT to develop.

Is there anything you think you are strong in that wasn't on the list?

If you had to pick just your top 3 strengths, what would you pick?

1. _____

2. _____

3. _____

If you had to pick just ONE strength you want to develop, what would you pick?

How would you describe your strengths?

Leaders

Imagine you are a tall, strong tree. You have grown strong and tall because you have lots of solid roots under the ground holding you up. This strong tree is a leader.

How are you a strong leader with a tall trunk, solid roots, and sturdy branches?

Strong, confident leaders know who they are, have people who love and support them, have passions, and encounter challenges and struggles.

Draw a picture of a tree below. Your tree should have roots and branches.
1. Fill the tree trunk with words that represent who you are.
2. Near the roots, list people who love you and support you.
3. Fill the branches with things you want to try and people you want to help.
4. Finally, the wind is the struggles and challenges that try to blow you over. Draw the wind and list a few struggles you are having now.

Journal Prompts

Why Journal Prompts?

Journaling is not merely a means of improving writing skills; it is a powerful self-reflective practice that encourages you to explore thoughts, emotions, and experiences.

Spend 5 minutes writing down your thoughts to the prompts to explore and reflect.

Prompts

There are lots of parts to your personality. What parts do you not show others? Why? What would happen if others saw that part of you?

"Be yourself; everyone else is already taken." - Oscar Wilde

How do you stay true to yourself?

If you could change one thing about yourself, what would it be and why?

"Our greatest weakness lies in giving up. The most certain way to succeed is always to try just one more time."
- Thomas Edison

Describe a time when you didn't give up.

When you see a glass of water where the water is halfway down the glass, do you say the glass is half full or half empty? Are you naturally a person who looks at the positives or looks at the challenges? Explain.

"Obstacles don't have to stop you. If you run into a wall, don't turn around and give up. Figure out how to climb it, go through it, or work around it." - Michael Jordan

What is an obstacle that hasn't stopped you? How did you overcome it?

If you were trapped on a deserted island, what is the one thing you would want to have with you? Explain.

What do you love best about yourself?

"I find that the harder I work, the more luck I seem to have." - Thomas Jefferson
How has this been true for you? Explain with an example from your life.

If you had unlimited money, what would you spend it on?

"I do know one thing about me: I don't measure myself by others' expectations or let others define my worth." - Sonia Sotomayor
How do you define yourself? How do you cope with other people's expectations of you?

Emotions themselves aren't good or bad; they are just feelings. How does this idea about emotions make you feel? Explain.

"I always try to start out with some type of goal. Then I work backward and think of what I need to do to get there, and give myself smaller goals that are more immediate." - Kristi Yamaguchi
Write a goal for yourself and then work backward to give yourself smaller goals to accomplish your big goal.

Prompts

What type of friend are you? Explain.

"The best advice I can give to anyone going through a rough patch is to never be afraid to ask for help." - Demi Lovato
Describe a time when you were going through a rough patch. How did you cope?

What do you value most in friendships? How do your friends show this in your friendships?

"The purpose of human life is to serve, and to show compassion and the will to help others." - Albert Schweitzer
How do you care for other people?

Describe a time when you had a big fight or conflict with someone. If it ended where you both felt good after the conflict, what happened? What did you say or do to resolve it? If it ended badly, imagine what you could have done to help resolve the conflict. What could you have said or done?

If you could spend the day with anyone (living today or from the past), who would it be and why? What would you want to do with them?

"I've learned that people will forget what you said, people will forget what you did, but people will never forget how you made them feel."
- Maya Angelou
How do you hope to make others feel when you are with them? Explain.

Describe a time when you were courageous. What happened?

Who do you surround yourself with? Do they lift you up or put you down? Explain.

"I learned that courage was not the absence of fear, but the triumph over it. The brave man is not he who does not feel afraid, but he who conquers that fear." - Nelson Mandela
Describe a time when you conquered a fear and showed courage."

"Real courage is doing the right thing when nobody's looking. Doing the unpopular thing because it's what you believe." - Justin Cronin
When did you do the unpopular thing because it was the right thing to do? What happened? How do you feel?"

Pretend your friend told you about their big struggle, but you haven't experienced what they are going through. How would you help them know you are there for them and care for them?

It is essential to be kind to yourself and others. Describe a time when you showed kindness to yourself. What did you do? What did you say to yourself?

Prompts

Describe a time when someone intentionally included you in a group or activity? How did they make you feel welcome?

"Diversity is not about how we differ. Diversity is about embracing each other's uniqueness." - Ola Joseph
What makes you unique? How can you (or do you) celebrate your uniqueness?

Describe a time when you felt like you didn't belong. How did it make you feel? How can you be a leader in social situations to help others avoid that feeling?

"Empathy grows as we learn." - Alice Miller
What is something you have learned that helps you understand people who are different from you?

What does respecting someone look like to you? Think about your actions, words, and thoughts.

Describe a time when you needed to apologize for something you did. What happened, and how did you apologize?

"You never really understand a person until you consider things from his point of view ... until you climb into his skin and walk around in it."
- Harper Lee in To Kill a Mockingbird
What do you think this quotation means? What does it mean to you?

If you could change anything about the world, what would you change and why?

"Every individual matters. Every individual has a role to play. Every individual makes a difference." - Jane Goodall
Think about someone in your life who you have a hard time relating to or connecting with. How does that person make a difference in the world? How does that person matter?

"I truly believe the only way we can create global peace is through not only educating our minds, but our hearts and our souls." - Malala Yousafzai
Brainstorm some ways you can educate your heart and soul about people who are different from you. How can you help create peace in your community and in the world?

Collaboration can inspire and connect you with others but can also be a struggle. When have you collaborated with others and felt inspired and connected? What happened?

"If you want to lift yourself up, lift up someone else." - Booker T. Washington
Describe a time when you encouraged someone else. What did you say? How did the person respond? How did you feel afterwards?

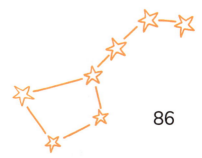

What is your favorite way to keep yourself healthy? (physically, emotionally, mentally, or spiritually)

"The mind is not a vessel to be filled but a fire to be ignited." - Plutarch. What is something you are passionate about that is a fire that's been ignited in you?

When you are super stressed out or anxious, what do you do that helps you feel better?

"Motivation is what gets you started. Habit is what keeps you going."
- Jim Ryun
What is a habit you want to start? How will you make it part of your daily routine?

"The beautiful thing about learning is that no one can take it away from you." - B.B. King
What is one thing you have learned in your life that you will never forget? How has it shaped your life or your thinking?

It can be hard to make big decisions. What is a big decision you had to make in your life? How did you decide on what to do?

"Give, but do not allow yourself to be used. Love, but do not allow your heart to be abused. Trust, but do not be naive. Listen to others, but do not lose yourself." - Doreen Virtue
Do you think this is good advice? Why or why not? Use your own experience in your answer.

Technology can be a huge benefit and help us live healthier lives, but it can also hinder us. How has technology improved your well-being?

It can be hard to balance our time. How do you keep a healthy balance in your life between technology, social media, after-school activities, friends, and family?

"The point is not to pay back kindness but to pass it on." - Julia Alvarez
How can you pass on kindness? How can this improve your own wellbeing and life?

Life can be a struggle. Who do you go to for help when you realize you are struggling? Why do you go to that person? Explain.

"A calm mind brings inner strength and self-confidence, so that's very important for good health." - Dalai Lama
How does a calm mind bring you strength and confidence? How do you calm your mind?

Projects

Kindness Challenge

How can you and your class make being kind contagious at your school and in your community?

Work with your class to create a 30-day Kindness Challenge for yourself.

For each day, fill in one way you (or you and the class together) can show kindness to your school, family, or community on the calendar on page 2.

Ideas:

- Bake someone treats.
- Do someone's laundry.
- Give someone a hug.
- Text a friend you haven't talked to in a while.
- Wash someone's car.
- Babysit, cat sit, or dog sit.
- Mow someone's lawn.
- Pick up trash by the side of the road or walking trail.
- Make care packages for the homeless or military.
- Bring donuts to the school administration in the morning.
- Leave positive sticky notes on people's lockers.

Kindness Challenge

	M	T	W	T	F	S	S
week 1							
week 2							
week 3							
week 4							

Use this sheet to check in during your Kindness Challenge to reflect on what you are noticing and learning.

Reflections after Week 1:

Reflections after Week 2:

Reflections after Week 3:

Reflections after Week 4:

Diversity Read-a-Thon

You and your class are challenged to a Diversity Read-a-Thon over the next month of school!

How many books can you read over the next 30 days that show diverse experiences, cultures, and places?

A Read-a-Thon is simply a reading challenge.

In this challenge, you must read as many WINDOW books as possible. You can pick novels, poetry, short stories, non-fiction, and even picture books! As long as the book is a window book for you, it counts!

Fill out the activity below to organize yourself and prepare for the Read-a-Thon!

Our class Read-a-Thon will take place

from _____

to _____.

My goal is to read _____ books!

> Remember, a **window** book is a book that focuses on an experience that is new to you. Perhaps a different time and place, the book is in a different country, or the main character has a very different lived experience than you.

Book title	This book was a window for me because...

I read _____ books!

As a class, we read _____ books!

What was your favorite book? Why?

What did you learn about yourself by reading these window books?

What did you learn about other experiences by reading these window books?

Self-Assessment

Self-Awareness Assessment

Name: ....

	Always	Sometimes	Never
I can identify my emotions	○	○	○
I understand how my emotions may affect my behavior	○	○	○
I use a growth mindset to do hard things	○	○	○
I am special and deserve love	○	○	○

I know my strengths and weaknesses.

○ ○ ○ ○ ○ ○ ○ ○ ○ ○
1   2   3   4   5   6   7   8   9   10

Not really.   Very much so!

What goal do you have to improve your self-awareness?

_____

_____

_____

_____

Self-Management Assessment

Name: _____

	Always	Sometimes	Never
I can manage emotions I feel	○	○	○
I can calm down and not hurt others or myself	○	○	○
I can set appropriate goals for myself	○	○	○
I can organize myself so I can turn things in on time	○	○	○

How well do you manage your emotions?

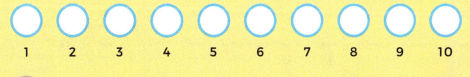

1 2 3 4 5 6 7 8 9 10

Not really.   Very much so!

What goal do you have to improve your self-management?

_____

_____

_____

_____

Relationship Skills Assessment

Name: ....

	Always	Sometimes	Never
I make friends easily	○	○	○
I can trust my friends	○	○	○
I can be flexible and compromise with others	○	○	○
I can ask for help when I need it	○	○	○

Are you good at working with other people?

○ ○ ○ ○ ○ ○ ○ ○ ○ ○
10 9 8 7 6 5 4 3 2 1

Yes! All the time! — This is hard for me.

What goal do you have to improve your relationship skills?

_____

_____

_____

_____

Social Awareness Assessment

Name: ....

	Always	Sometimes	Never
I have friends who are different than me	○	○	○
I know others can see things differently than me	○	○	○
I listen to others to try to understand them	○	○	○
I respect everyone even if I don't agree with them	○	○	○

How often do you thank people in your life?

○ 10   ○ 9   ○ 8   ○ 7   ○ 6   ○ 5   ○ 4   ○ 3   ○ 2   ○ 1

♥ All the time!   ☹ Not often.

What goal do you have to improve your social awareness?

_____

_____

_____

_____

Responsible Decision-Making Assessment

Name: ....

	Always	Sometimes	Never
I like to learn new things	○	○	○
I am a good problem solver	○	○	○
I understand consequences	○	○	○
I understand my decisions can affect others	○	○	○

How well do you manage your emotions?

○ 1 ○ 2 ○ 3 ○ 4 ○ 5 ○ 6 ○ 7 ○ 8 ○ 9 ○ 10

☹ Not very well. ❤ Very well.

What goal do you have to improve your responsible decision-making skills?

_____

_____

_____

_____

Printed in the USA
CPSIA information can be obtained
at www.ICGtesting.com
JSHW051346041123
51224JS00036B/132